Farm Animals

SHEEP

Rachael Bell

Heinemann
LIBRARY

www.heinemann.co.uk
Visit our website to find out more information about Heinemann Library books.

To order:

 Phone 44 (0) 1865 888066

 Send a fax to 44 (0) 1865 314091

Visit the Heinemann Bookshop at www.heinemann.co.uk to browse our catalogue and order online.

First published in Great Britain by Heinemann Library,
Halley Court, Jordan Hill, Oxford OX2 8EJ,
a division of Reed Educational and Professional Publishing Ltd.
Heinemann is a registered trademark of Reed Educational and Professional Publishing Ltd.

OXFORD MELBOURNE AUCKLAND
JOHANNESBURG BLANTYRE GABORONE
IBADAN PORTSMOUTH (NH) USA CHICAGO

Designed by AMR
Originated by Ambassador Litho ltd
Printed by South China Printing in Hong Kong/China

ISBN 0 431 13332 8 (hardback)   ISBN 0 431 13337 9 (paperback)
05 04 03 02 01   05 04 03 02 01
10 9 8 7 6 5 4 3 2 1   10 9 8 7 6 5 4 3 2 1

British Library Cataloguing in Publication Data

Bell, Rachael, 1972–
    Sheep. – (Farm animals) (Take-off!)
    1.Sheep – Juvenile literature
    I.Title
    636.3

Acknowledgements

Agripicture p 21/Peter Dean; J Allan Cash Ltd, p 27; Anthony Blake Photo Library p 23/Sue Atkinson; Bruce Coleman pp 8/Jorg & Petra Wegner, 18/Stephen Bond; Farmers Weekly Picture Library pp 11, 13, 19; Holt Studios pp 4 l/Richard Anthony, 12 & 14/Wayne Hutchinson, 15/Primrose Peacock, 24/ Gordon Roberts; Chris Honeywell p 25; Images of Nature/FLPA pp 4 r/Tony Hamblin, 5/I. Lee Rue, 6/Derek A. Robinson, 16/Peter Dean, 17/M. J. Thomas, 20/Peter Dean; Martin Sookias, p 22; Lynn M Stone pp 9, 10, 28; Tony Stone Images pp 7/Philip H. Coblentz, 26/Anthony Cassidy, 29/David Woodfall.

Cover photograph reproduced with permission of Oxford Scientific Films.

Our thanks to Sue Graves and Hilda Reed for their advice and expertise in the preparation of this book.

Every effort has been made to contact copyright holders of any material reproduced in this book. Any omissions will be rectified in subsequent printings if notice is given to the publishers.

Contents

What do sheep look like?   4

On the sheep farm   6

Adult sheep   8

Young sheep   10

Where are sheep kept?   12

What do sheep eat?   14

How do farmers keep sheep healthy?   16

How do sheep sleep?   18

Who looks after sheep?   20

What are sheep kept for?   22

What else are sheep kept for?   24

Other kinds of sheep farm   26

Factfile   28

Glossary   30

More books to read   32

Index   32

Any words appearing in the text in bold, **like this**, are explained in the Glossary.

What do sheep look like?

long, curly coat

short, smooth coat

Sheep can have long or short coats.

Most sheep are white, but they can also be black
or dark brown. Their coats may be long and
curly or short and smooth.

Sheep were first kept by people
in Asia, 9000 years ago!

horns

This Bighorn sheep lives wild in North America.

Farmers choose sheep that suit where they live, so most sheep in one area look the same. Some sheep live wild, like this Bighorn sheep in North America.

The Bighorn is very good at climbing snow-covered rocks. Its woolly coat keeps it warm.

On the sheep farm

pasture

There are many sheep on this farm.

sheep

On this farm, the farmer keeps many sheep. He also has a sheep-dog. The sheep-dog is a working animal and is kept outside in the farmyard.

> Sheep that live in fields are called lowland sheep, and sheep that live on higher land are called hill sheep.

farmhouse

straw bales

crop

Crops are grown on this sheep farm, too.

Most of the land on the farm is **pasture** for the sheep to graze on. The farmer grows **cereals** like wheat and oats on the rest of the land. These are sold to make food for people.

Adult sheep

lamb   ewe   tail

udder

The lamb drinks milk from its mother's udder.

The **female** sheep is called a **ewe**. Ewes can have up to three lambs each year. They take good care of the lambs.

> The ewe has two **teats** on her udder, so two lambs can drink milk from their mother at the same time.

jaw   eye

Rams use their horns
to fight off other rams.

horn

hoof

The **male** sheep is called a ram. Some rams have horns. They can use them to fight off other rams and **protect** the ewes.

Young sheep

This lamb is bleating for its mother.

lamb

Baby sheep are called lambs. They can walk within minutes of being born. Lambs make a high-sounding noise, called bleating.

A lamb is born five months after its parents have **mated**.

10

lambs

ewe

This sheep has two lambs.

When lambs are very young, they feed on milk from their mother. After 14 weeks, the lambs start to eat grass and other food.

Where are sheep kept?

A sheep's fleece keeps it warm even when there is snow on the ground.

fleece

Sheep spend most of their lives outdoors. They are very tough animals. A sheep's thick **fleece** keeps it warm, even in freezing weather.

ewe

straw

The sheep are kept inside during lambing time.

At **lambing time**, most sheep are kept in a barn with deep **straw** on the floor. The **ewe** and her lambs go outside again when the lambs are about three weeks old.

Lambs can eat grass for the first time when they are three weeks old.

13

What do sheep eat?

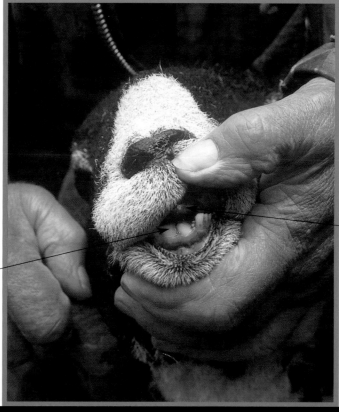

teeth in bottom jaw

pad in top of mouth

A sheep's mouth is ideal for nibbling short grass.

Sheep's mouths are made for nibbling short grass. They bite off grass between their bottom front teeth and upper **pad**, then swallow it. Later they **chew the cud** between their back teeth.

A farmer can work out how old a sheep is by counting its teeth. It gets two new teeth each year for four years.

14

sheep

feed trough

In winter, sheep eat hay and ewe nuts.

In winter when the grass stops growing quickly, sheep eat **hay** and **ewe** nuts. Ewe nuts are made from **cereals**. Sheep drink water from **troughs** all year round.

How do farmers keep sheep healthy?

These sheep eat fresh grass to keep them healthy.

Sheep catch **diseases** and **parasites** very easily. They get them from each other and from the ground. The best way to keep sheep healthy is to make sure they have lots of space in open **pastures**.

sheep

sheep-dip

farm worker

Once a year, sheep are dipped in a special liquid.

Farmers take good care of their sheep. They dip the sheep in a special liquid to kill any parasites. They also give the sheep **injections** against diseases.

To make sure that the whole of the sheep has been dipped, the farm worker will duck the sheep's head under the liquid, too.

17

How do sheep sleep?

These sheep have found a sheltered area to rest.

As it gets dark, sheep gather together. They find an area out of the wind and rain and lie down with their backs to the wind.

Sheep like to stay close to each other, so they often follow each other around.

pasture

Sheep like to graze.

Sheep sleep with their eyes closed. If you disturb them, they wake up and run off. Sometimes they **graze**, too, but they soon lie down again to rest.

Who looks after sheep?

The sheep-dog helps the shepherd to move the sheep.

sheep-dog

The **shepherd** checks the sheep every day in the field with his sheep-dog. The dog runs around the sheep to collect them up and move them to the next field.

A shepherd calls or uses different whistles to tell the sheep-dog what to do.

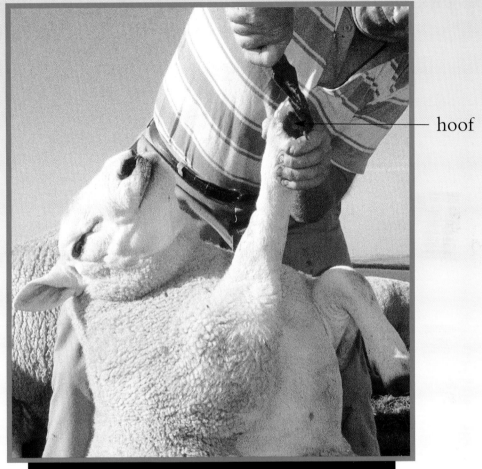

hoof

This sheep is having its hooves trimmed.

The farmer and his shepherd look after the **ewes** when they are inside. Sometimes they trim the sheep's **hooves**. This is a bit like having your nails cut.

What are sheep kept for?

lamb chop

lamb joints

The meat from sheep is called lamb.

Most farms keep sheep for their meat. The meat from sheep is called lamb. It can be used in many different dishes.

Many people like to eat roast lamb.

roast lamb

lemon

rosemary

The main cuts of meat from a lamb are the shoulder, leg or lamb chop. This is a roast leg of lamb. It was cooked with the **herb** called rosemary.

What else are sheep kept for?

sheep-shearer

electric shears

fleece

A sheep's fleece is sheared off with electric shears.

Sheep are also kept for their wool. A sheep's **fleece** is **sheared** off. This is a bit like having a hair cut! The fleece is sent to a factory to be cleaned and spun into wool.

The finest wool comes from Merino sheep.

Feta

Halloumi

Roquefort

All these cheeses have been made from ewes' milk.

Some farms also keep sheep for their creamy milk. They make special cheeses and yoghurt from it. Roquefort is a famous French blue cheese made from **ewes**' milk.

Roquefort is kept in caves before it is sold around the world.

25

Other kinds of sheep farm

These sheep live high in the mountains.

shepherd

In some parts of the world, farmers keep sheep high up in the mountains. The **shepherd** moves around with his sheep.

Hill sheep are thinner than lowland sheep, and they have longer legs, too!

There are thousands of sheep on an Australian sheep station.

In Australia, big sheep farms are called sheep stations. They have many thousands of sheep. The sheep are left alone for most of the year, until they are rounded up for market.

Factfile

Sheep live together in a **flock**. If one sheep moves, the others follow.

Sheep like to live in a flock.

Lambs have eight milk teeth when they are born. Each year two teeth fall out and are replaced by adult teeth. After a few years, even the adult teeth start to fall out.

A lamb's tail is docked soon after it is born. This means that the farmer puts a tight rubber ring on the tail to make it fall off. Docking the tail does not hurt a lamb at all. It is is done to stop the tail getting dirty underneath.

Sometimes a farmer needs a ewe to feed a lamb that is not hers. He holds the lamb so that the ewe cannot see or smell it. Usually, the ewe lets the lamb feed. If a ewe will not feed a lamb, the farmer's family feeds it with a bottle.

milk   bottle

This lamb has to be bottle-fed with milk.

Sheep's fleeces have been used for wool for more than 3000 years. In the old days, a spinning wheel was used to turn fleece into wool.

Sheep's wool has a natural oil in it called lanolin, which is used in lots of products such as soap and handcream. Look at the labels on some of those products to see if they have lanolin in them.

29

Glossary

a
b
c
d
e
f
g
h
i
j
k
l
m
n
o
p
q
r
s
t
u
v
w
x
y
z

cereals	plants like wheat, oats and barley, which are often made into breakfast food
chew the cud	bring food back up into the mouth from the stomach, to chew it again
crop	plant that the farmer grows in his fields
diseases	illnesses
ewe	female or mother sheep
female	girl or mother animal
fleece	sheep's coat of wool
flock	group of sheep that live together
graze	eat grass in a field
hay	grass that is cut and dried
herb	plant that is used in cooking to add flavour
hooves	hard pads of the sheep's feet
injection	special medicine which is given through a needle
lambing time	when the lambs are born
male	boy or father animal
mate	when a male and a female animal come together to produce young
milk teeth	first teeth

pad	hard area in a sheep's mouth
parasites	little animals that live on bigger animals and usually harm them
pasture	grass in a field that animals graze on
protect	keep safe
shear	cut off a sheep's fleece in one bundle
shepherd	person who looks after sheep
straw	thick, dried stalks of crops
teats	the parts of the sheep's udder where the lambs suck the milk
trough	food or water container for animals
udder	the part of the sheep's body that contains milk

a
b
c
d
e
f
g
h
i
j
k
l
m
n
o
p
q
r
s
t
u
v
w
x
y
z

More books to read

Babe the Sheep-pig,
Dick King-Smith, Longman, 2000

Encyclopedia of Animals of the World,
Dorling Kindersley, 1999

Index

Australia 27

ewe 8, 9, 13, 21, 25, 29

cheese 25

docking 28

eating 11, 14, 15

fleece 12, 24, 29

lambs 8, 10, 11, 13, 22, 28, 29

meat 22, 23

milk 8, 11, 25

ram 9

sheep-dog 6, 20

shepherd 20, 21, 26

sleep 18, 19

teeth 14, 28

wool 24, 29

a
b
c
d
e
f
g
h
i
j
k
l
m
n
o
p
q
r
s
t
u
v
w
x
y
z